THE PHILLIP KEVEREN SERIES   PIANO SOLO

CLASSICAL FOLK

CONTENTS

— PIANO LEVEL —
LATE INTERMEDIATE/EARLY ADVANCED

ISBN 1-4234-0783-0

HAL•LEONARD®
CORPORATION
7777 W. BLUEMOUND RD. P.O. BOX 13819 MILWAUKEE, WI 53213

Visit Hal Leonard Online at
www.halleonard.com

PREFACE

The title of this folio was suggested to me by one of my colleagues at Hal Leonard. The concept sounded intriguing. An earlier publication in this series, *Classical Jazz*, applied jazz stylings to classical themes. This time around, we are applying classical stylings to folk themes. If you are not entirely confused, please read on!

In this collection we have compiled folk tunes from around the world, some well-known, others more obscure, all of them beautiful in their own right. The arrangements cover a wide variety of styles, with each theme developing in a manner that seems most natural for its character. In the end, I hope we have created a folio of pianistic settings that will bring pleasure to many players and listeners.

Sincerely,
Phillip Keveren

BIOGRAPHY

Phillip Keveren, a multi-talented keyboard artist and composer, has composed original works in a variety of genres from piano solo to symphonic orchestra. Mr. Keveren gives frequent concerts and workshops for teachers and their students in the United States, Canada, Europe, and Asia. Mr. Keveren holds a B.M. in composition from California State University Northridge and a M.M. in composition from the University of Southern California.

THE BAMBOO FLUTE

Chinese Folksong
Arranged by Phillip Keveren

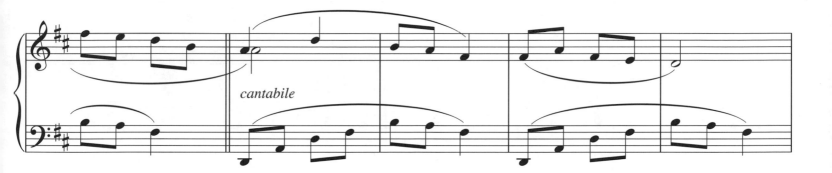

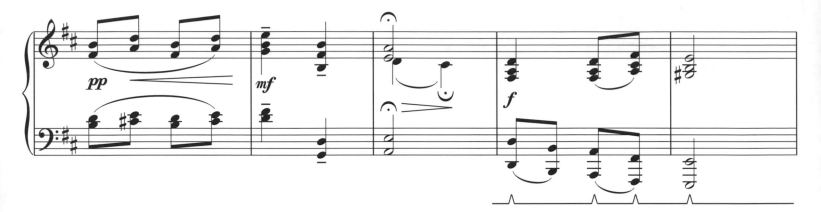

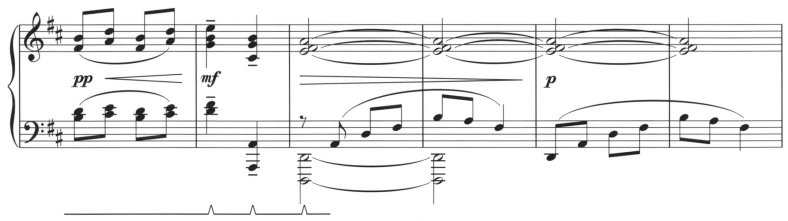

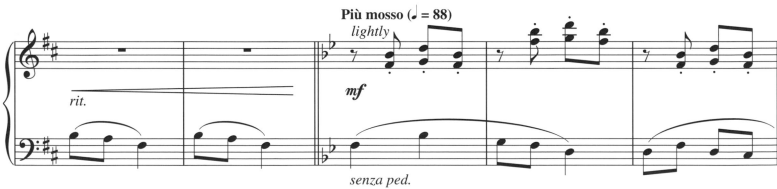

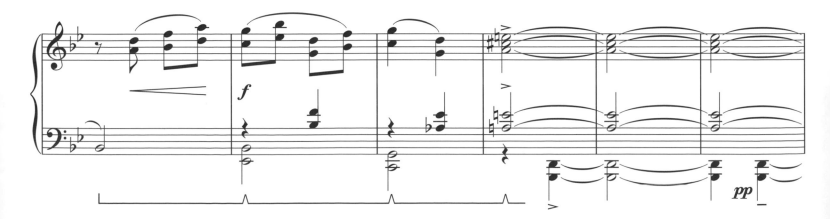

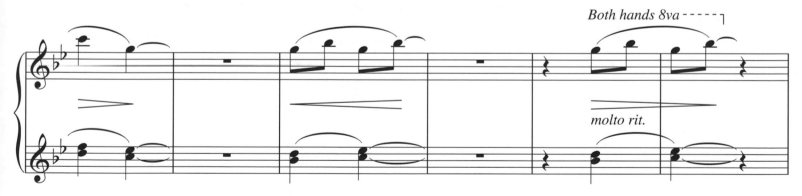

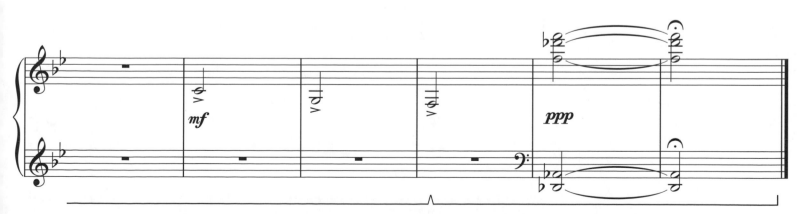

BARBARA ALLEN

Traditional English
Arranged by Phillip Keveren

Slowly, mysteriously (♩ = 69)

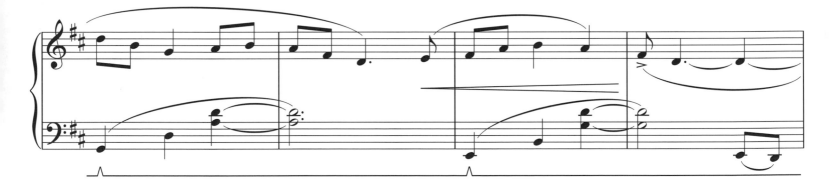

Gently flowing (♩ = 84)

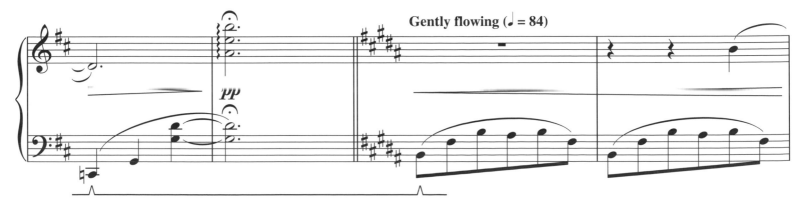

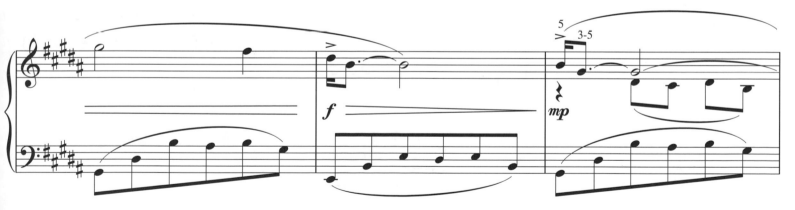

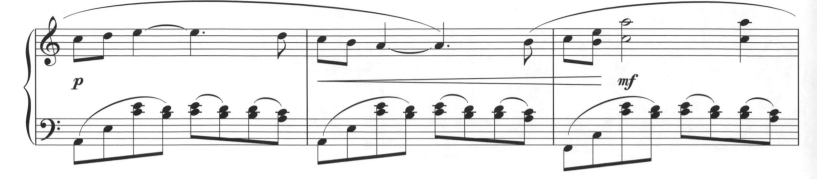

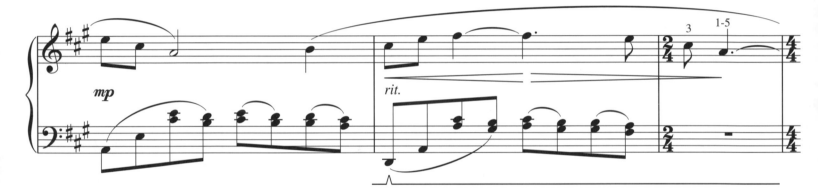

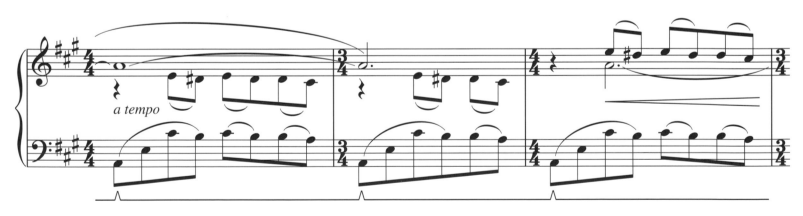

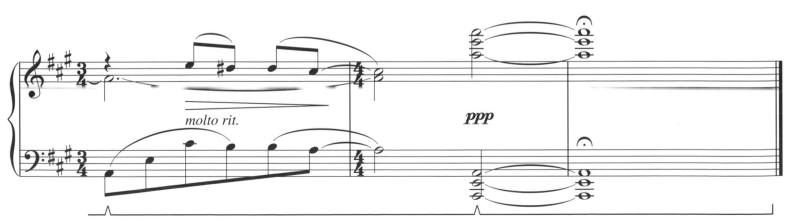

THE GALWAY PIPER

Irish Folksong
Arranged by Phillip Keveren

Spirited (♩ = 116)

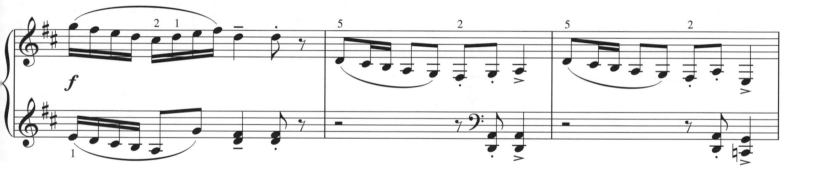

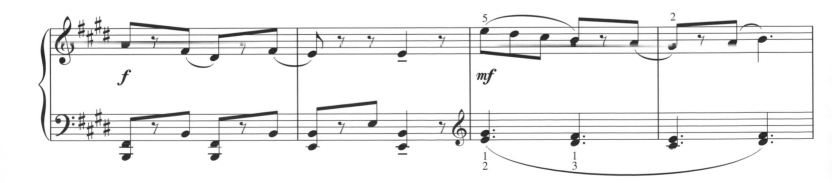

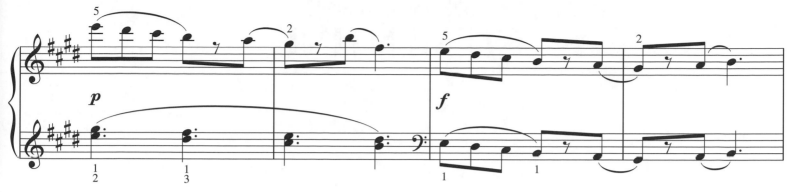

(Oh, My Darling)
CLEMENTINE

Words and Music by
PERCY MONTROSE
Arranged by Phillip Keveren

13

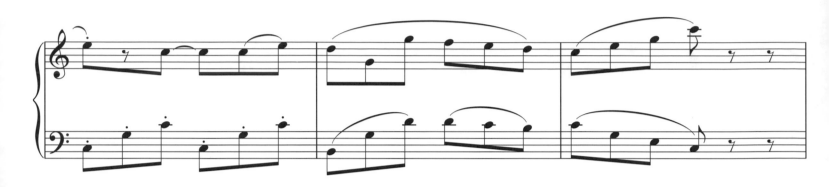

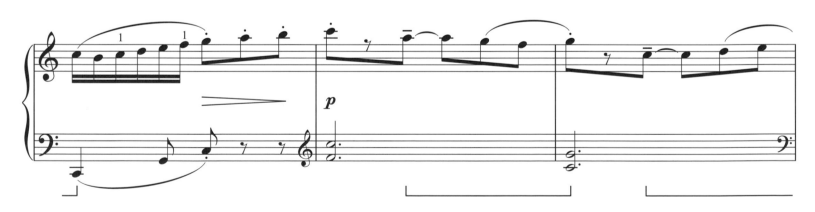

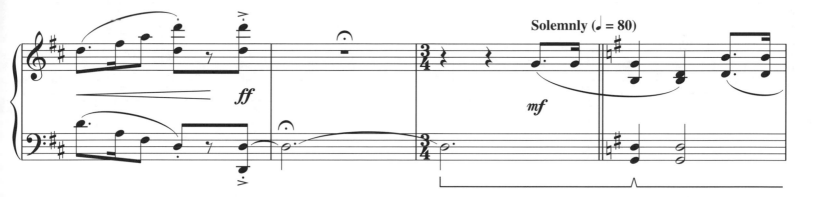

DU, DU LIEGST MIR IM HERZEN
(You, You Weigh on My Heart)

German Folksong
Arranged by Phillip Keveren

Moderate Waltz (♩ = 184)

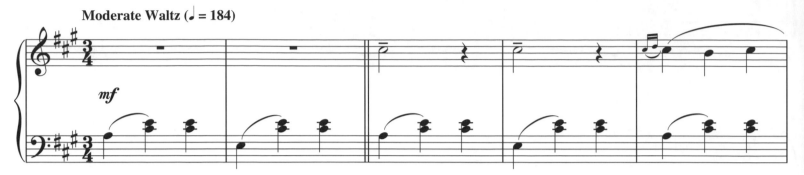

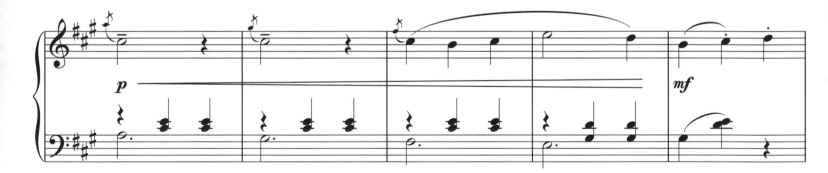

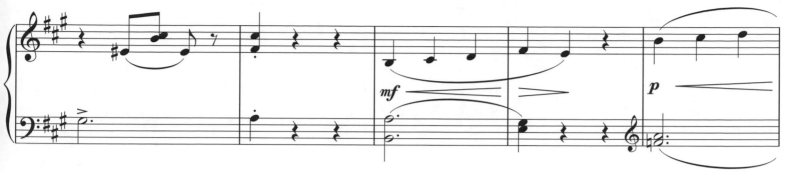

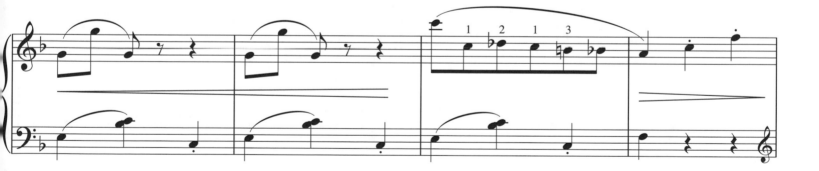

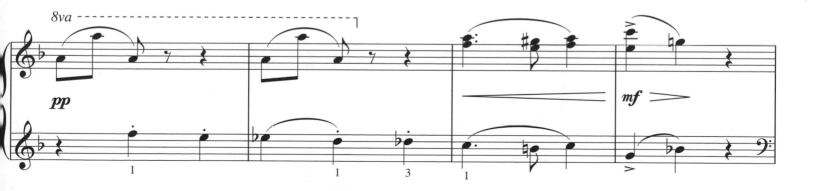

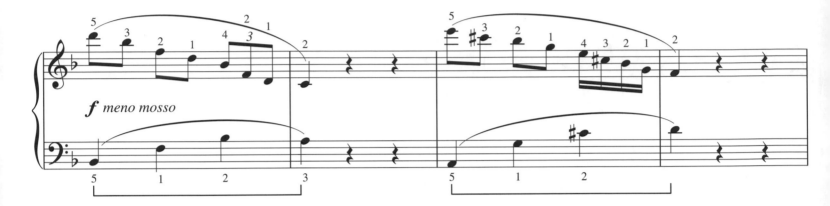

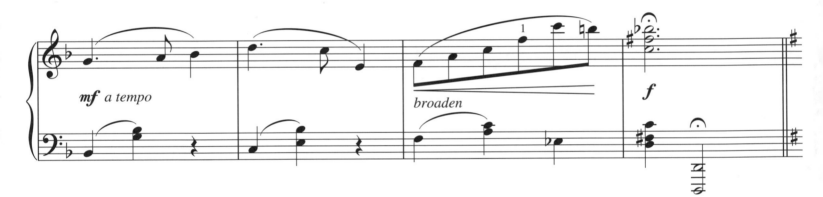

With grandeur (♩ = 168)

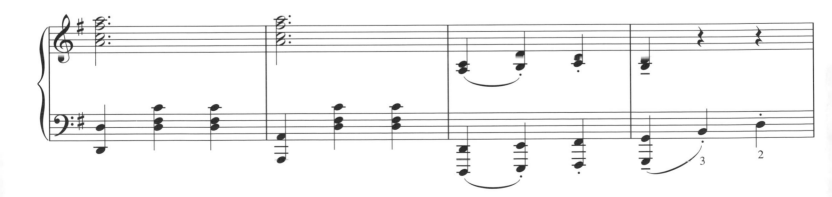

Slowly, tenderly (♩ = 92)

Tempo I

FRÈRE JACQUES
(Are You Sleeping?)

Traditional
Arranged by Phillip Keveren

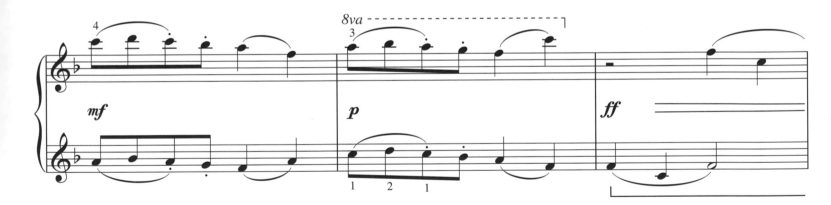

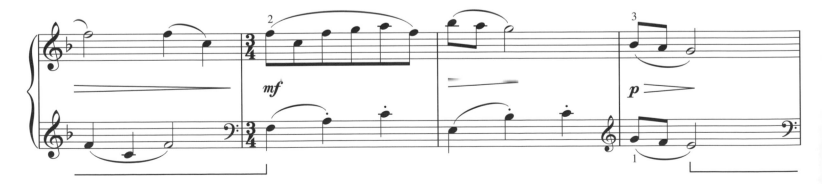

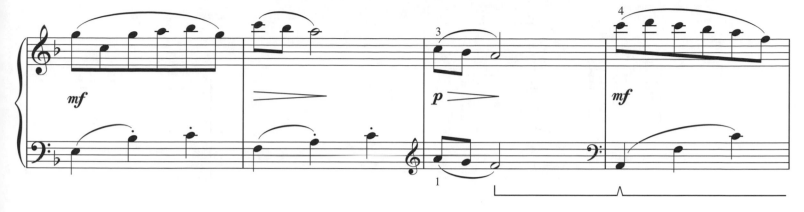

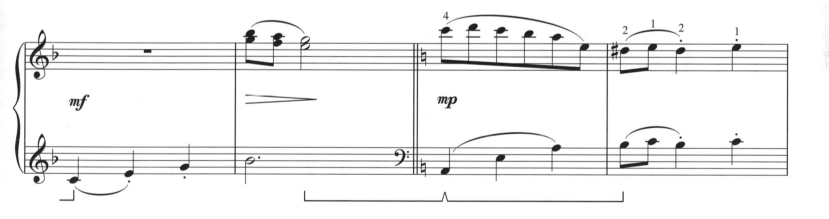

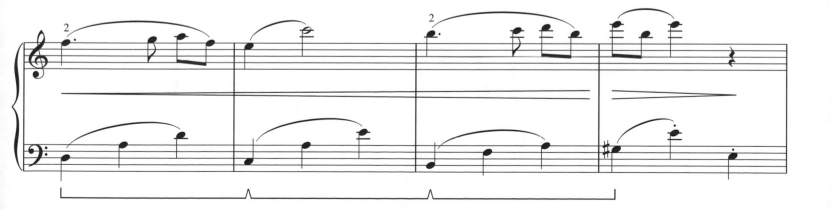

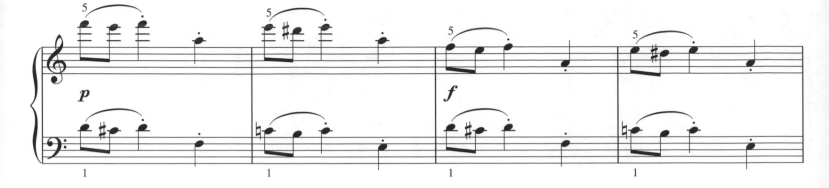

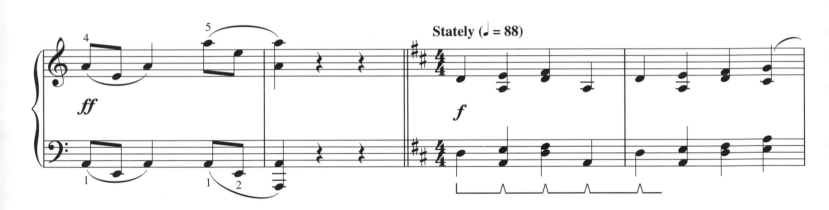

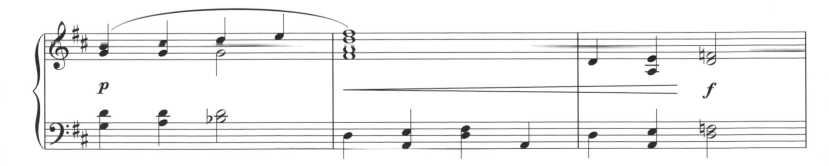

Briskly (♩. = 120)

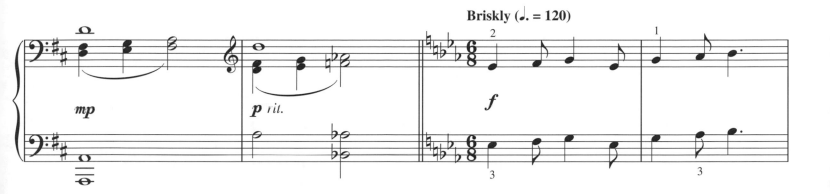

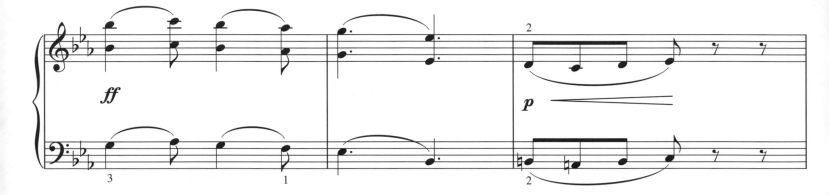

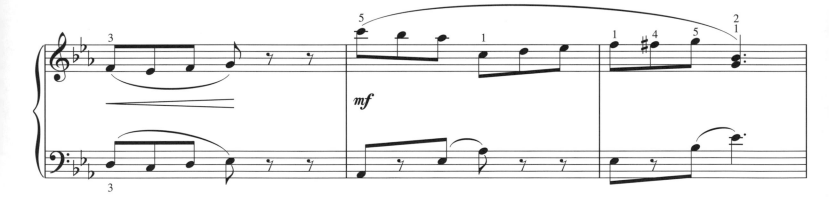

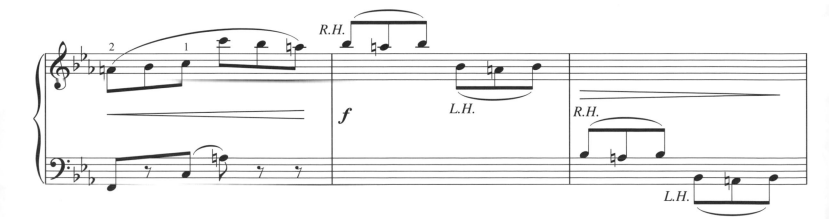

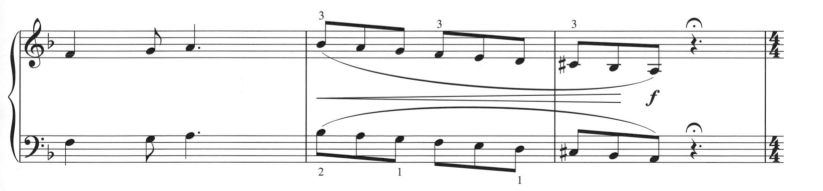

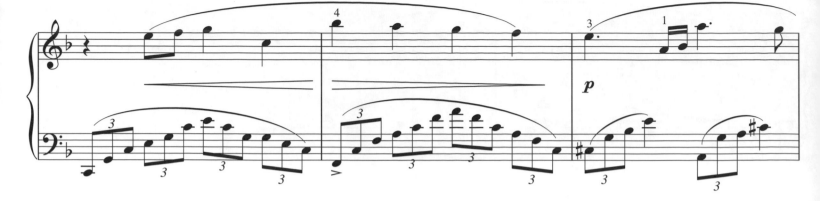

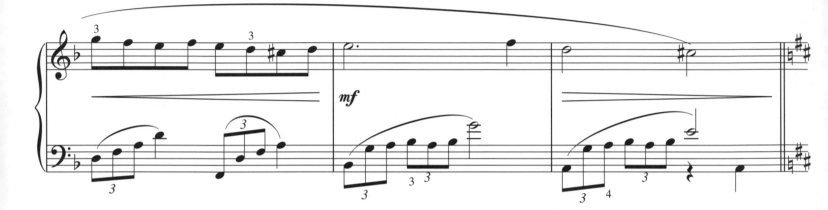

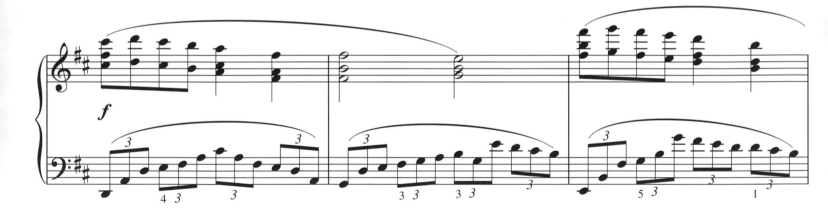

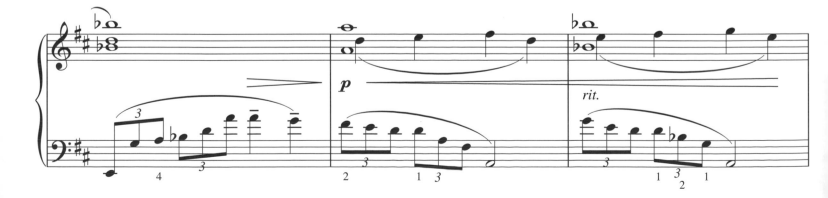

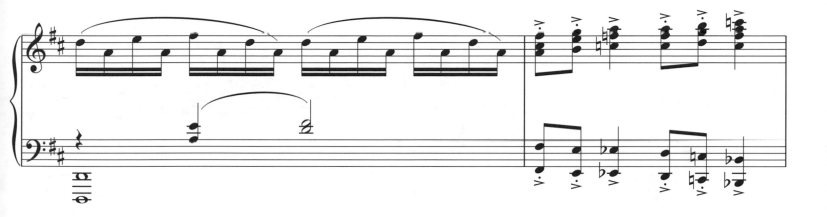

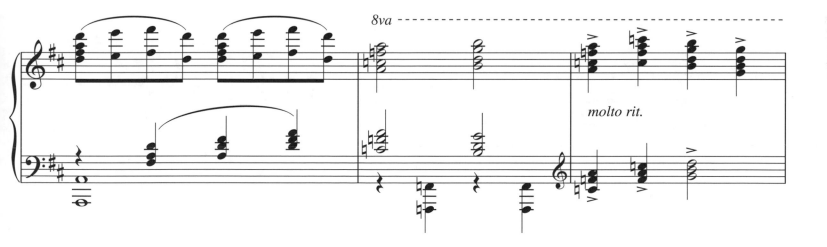

GREENSLEEVES

16th Century Traditional English
Arranged by Phillip Keveren

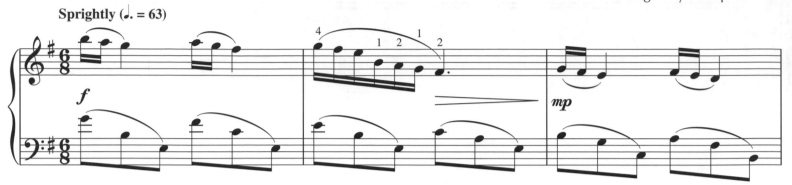

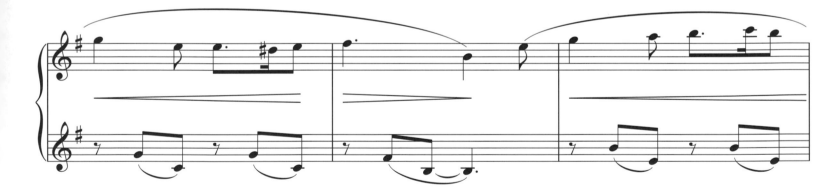

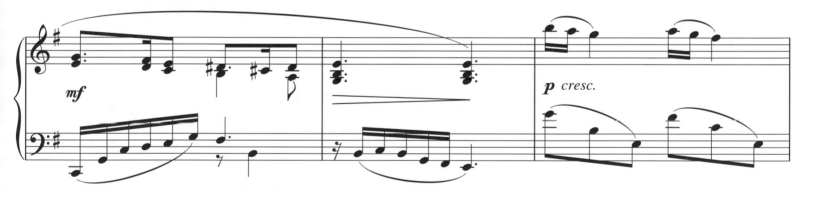

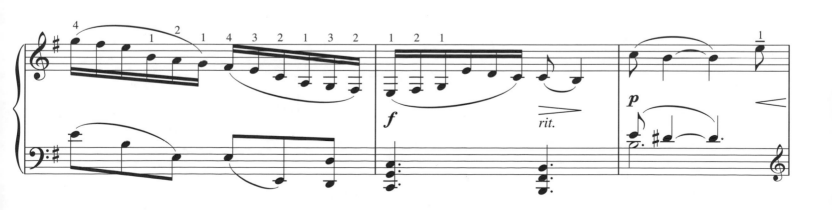

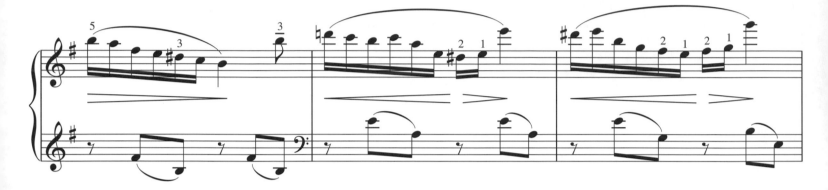

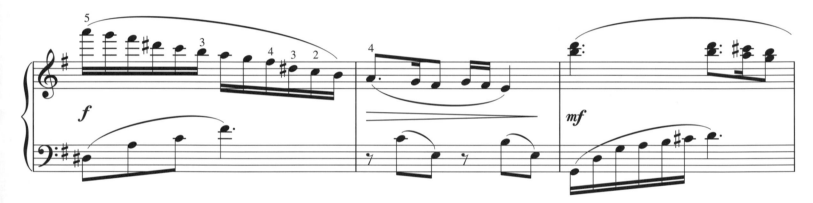

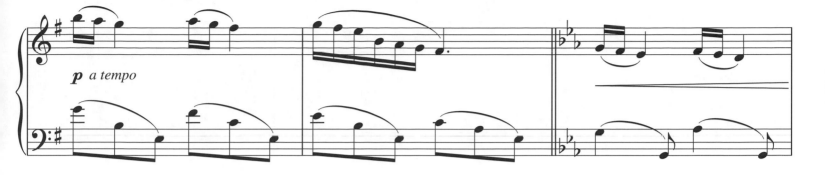

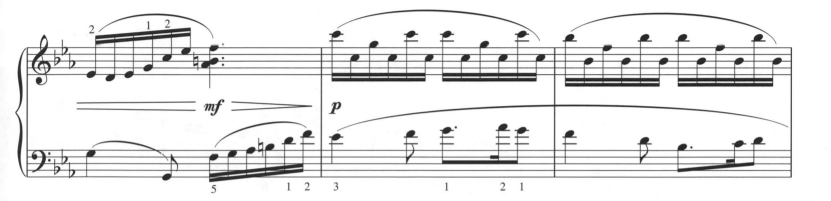

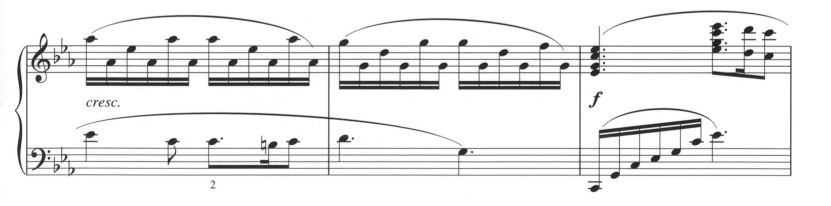

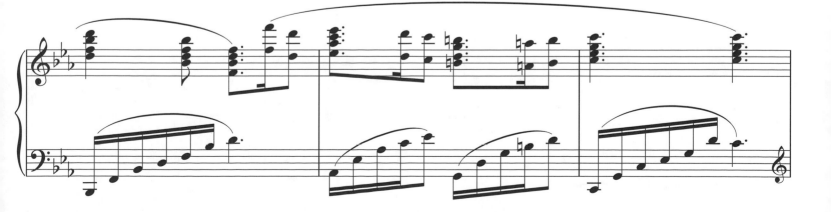

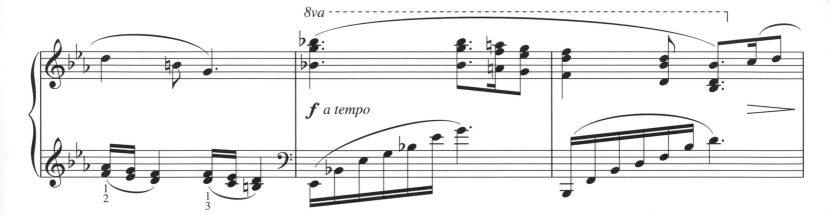

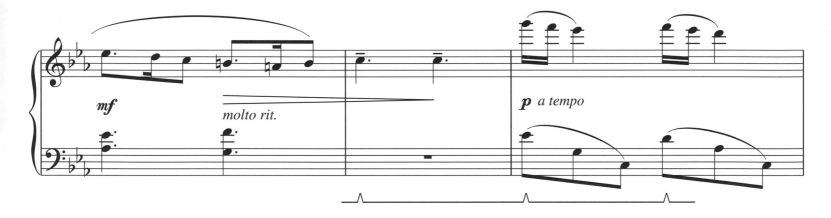

HATIKVAH
(With Hope)

Traditional Hebrew Melody
Lyrics by N.H. IMBER
Arranged by Phillip Keveren

Andante espressivo (♩ = 76)

With pedal

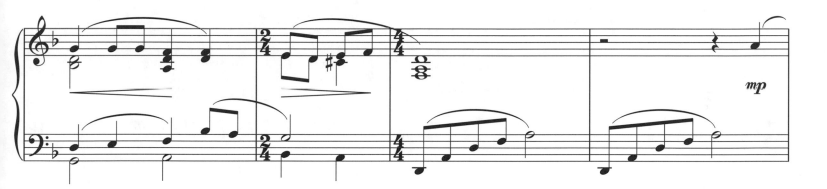

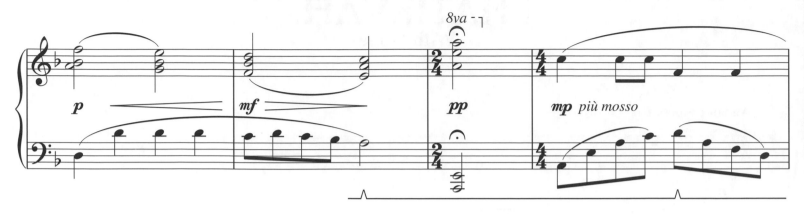

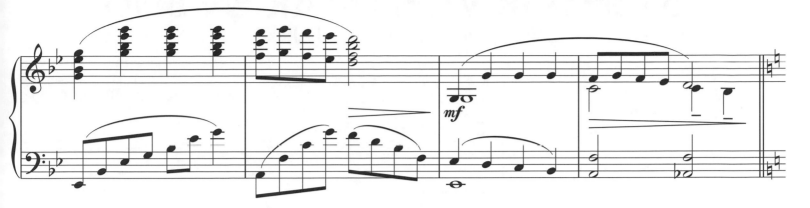

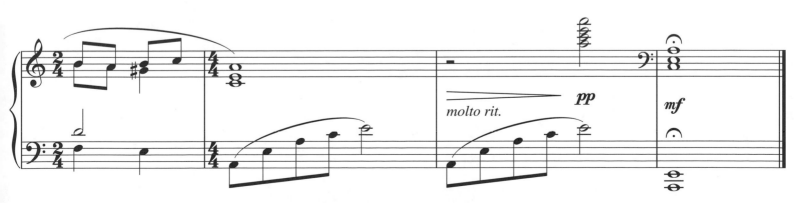

HIST, HYOR VEJEN SLÄR EN BUGT
(There, On Down the Road Ahead)

Lyrics by HANS CHRISTIAN ANDERSEN
Danish Folk Melody
Arranged by Phillip Keveren

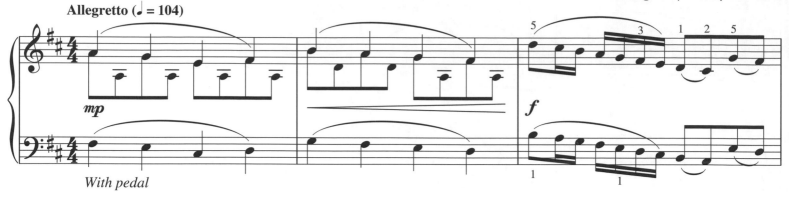

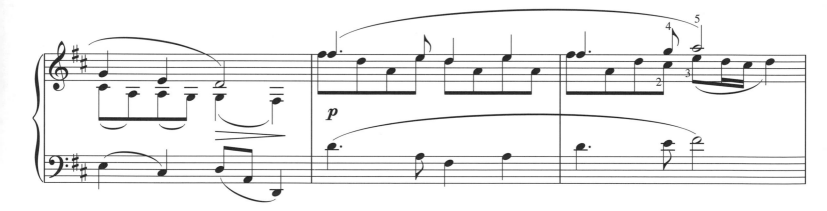

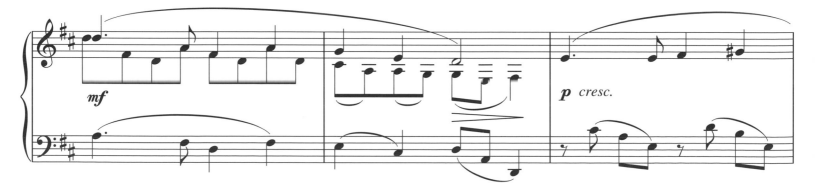

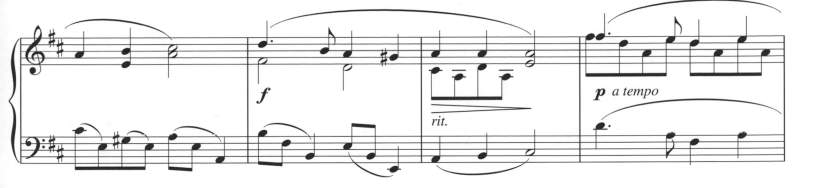

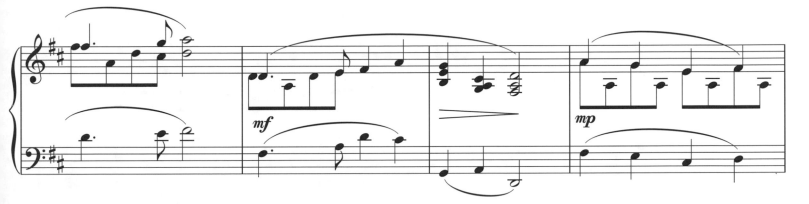

Tranquil (♩ = 88)

Tempo I (♩ = 104)

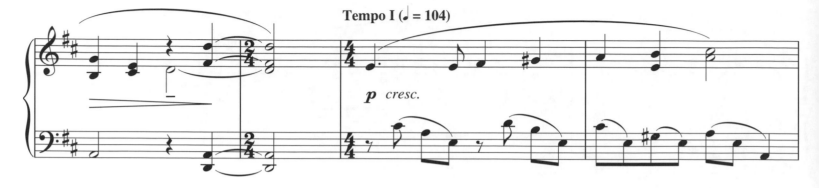

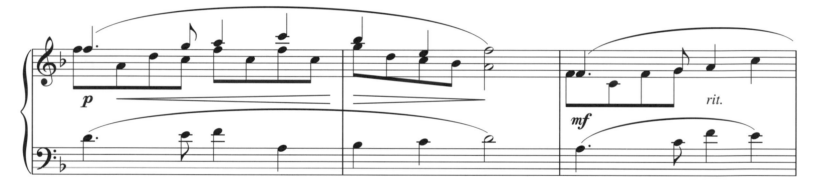

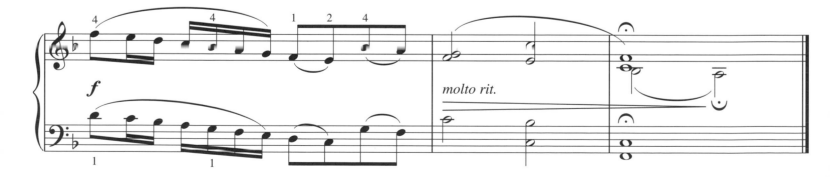

KRAKOWIAK
(Darling Maiden, Hark, I Ask Thee)

Polish Folksong
Arranged by Phillip Keveren

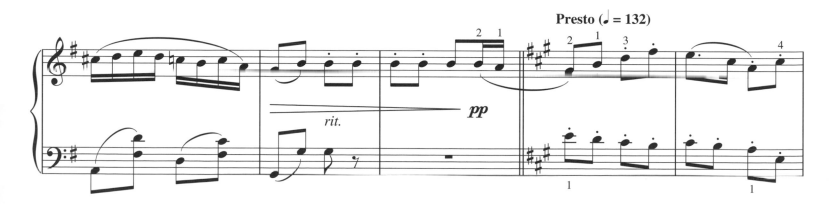

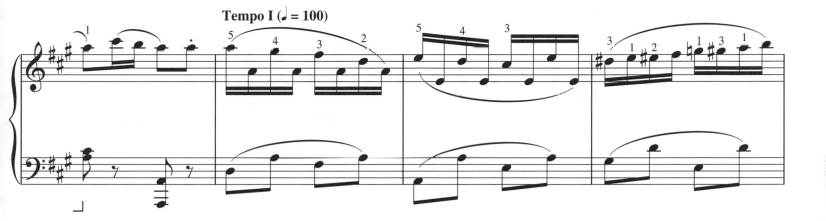

JACOB'S LADDER

African-American Spiritual
Arranged by Phillip Keveren

Lento (♩ = 66)

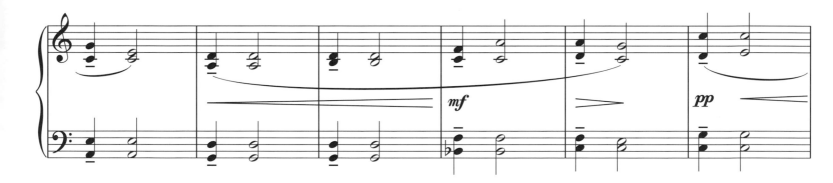

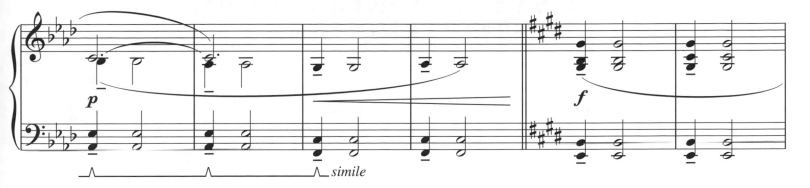

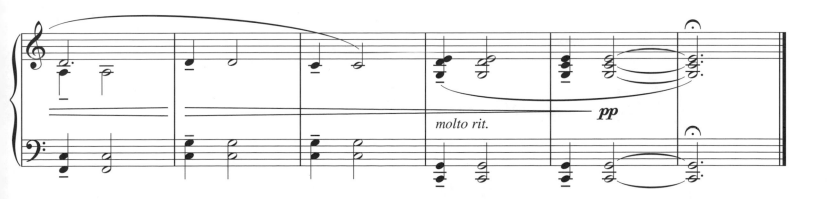

LA VERA SORRENTINA
(The Fair Maid of Sorrento)

Italian Folksong
Arranged by Phillip Keveren

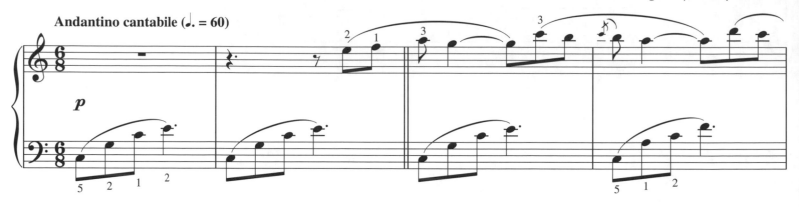

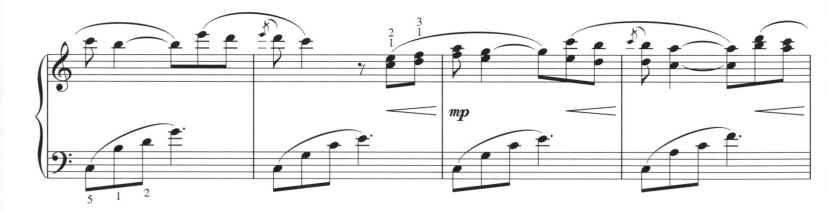

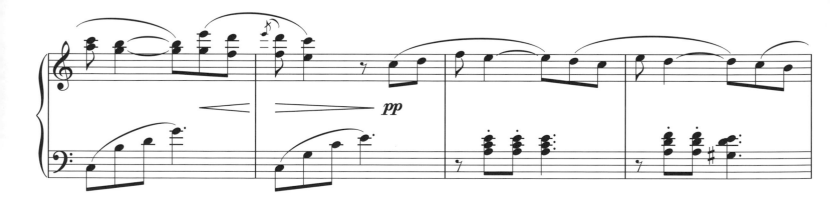

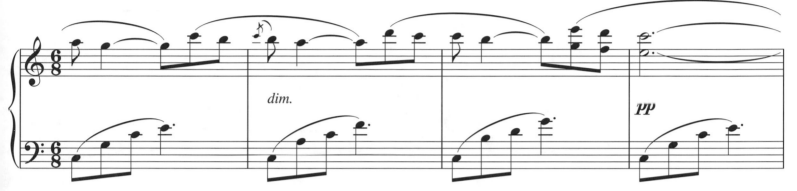

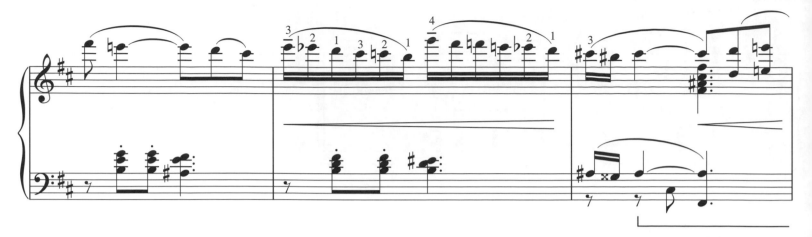

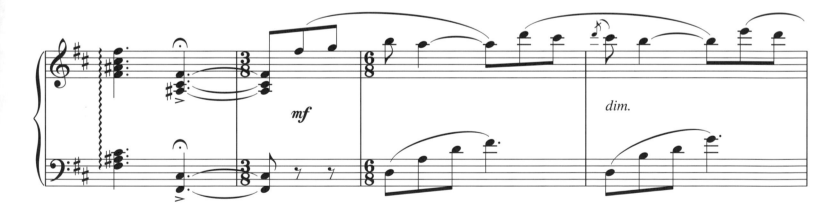

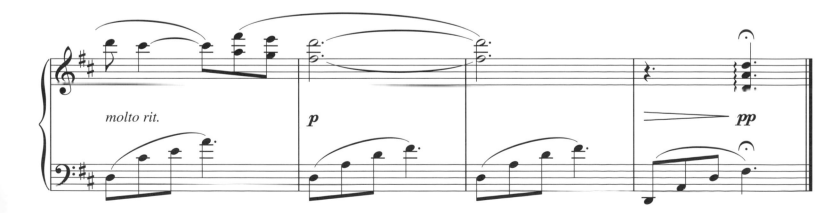

O WALY, WALY

English Folksong
Arranged by Phillip Keveren

Slowly, ringing (♩ = 52)

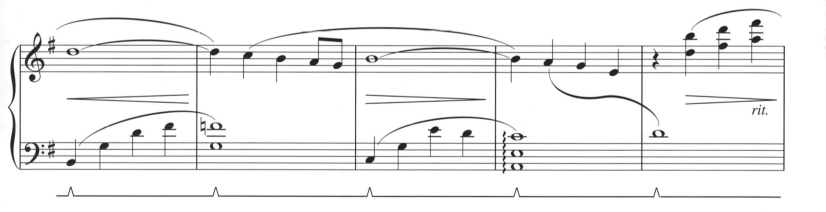

Flowing gracefully (♪ = 126)

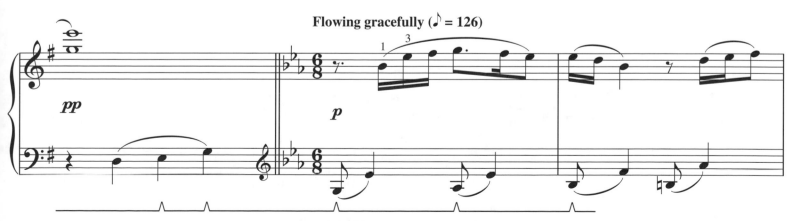

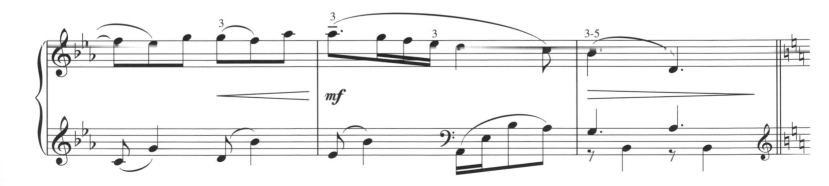

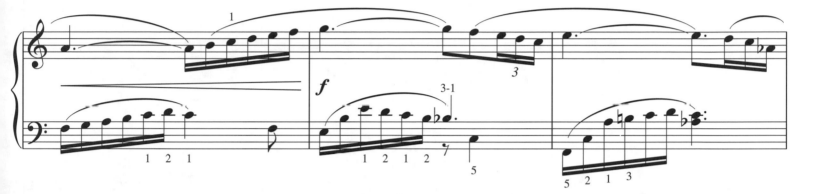

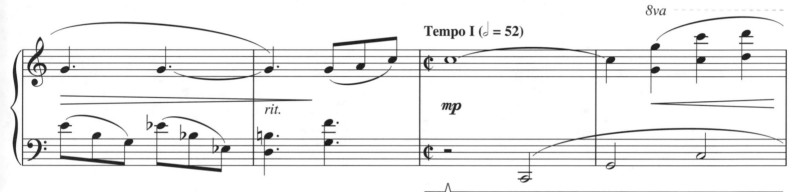

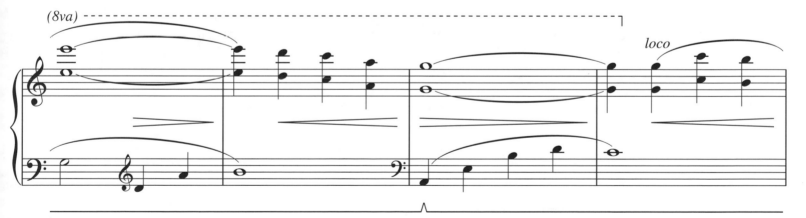

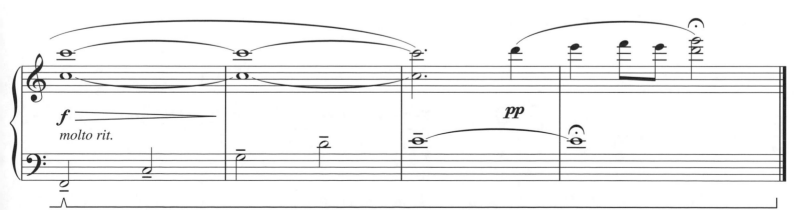

WHEN JOHNNY COMES MARCHING HOME

Words and Music by
PATRICK SARSFIELD GILMORE
Arranged by Phillip Keveren

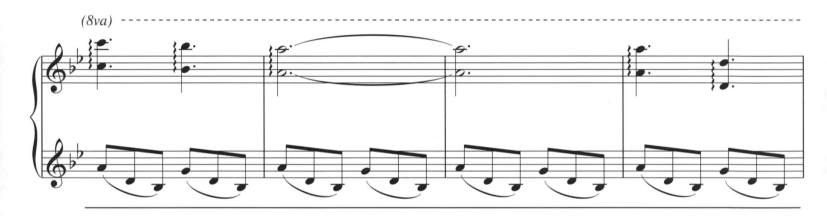

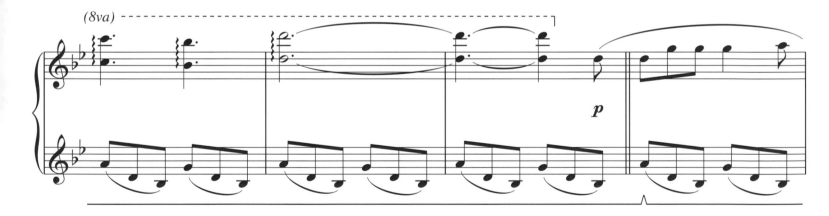

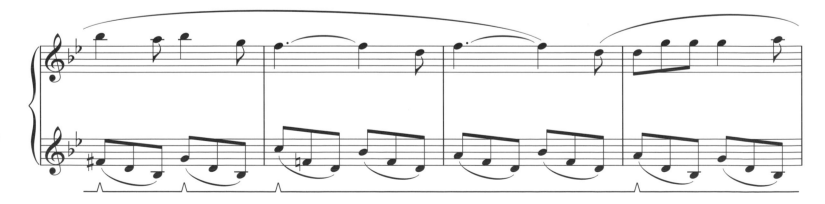

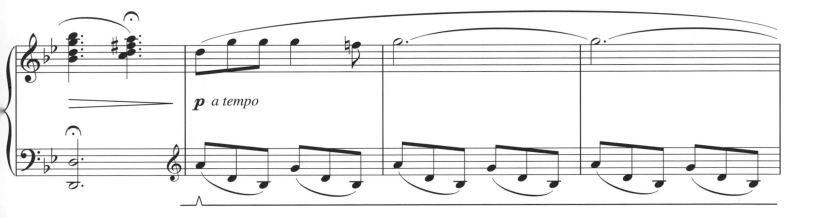

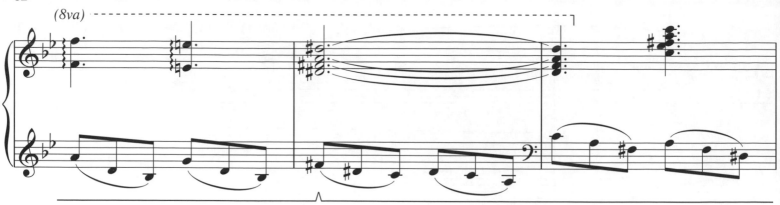

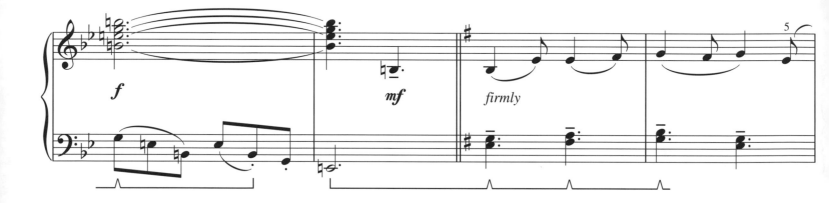

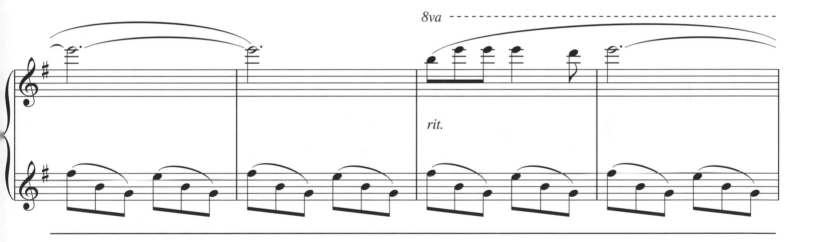

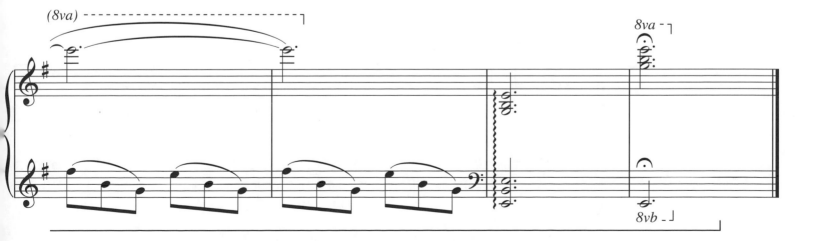

SWING LOW, SWEET CHARIOT

Traditional Spiritual
Arranged by Phillip Keveren

Freely, with deep expression (♩ = 72)

with a gentle lilt

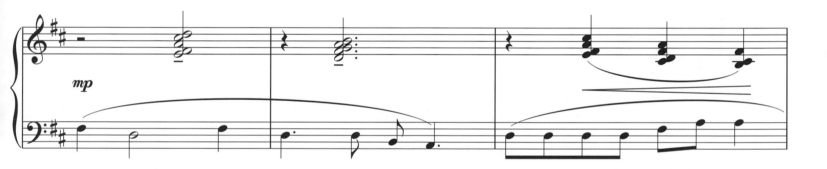

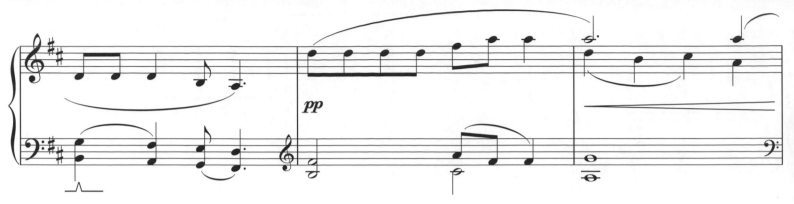

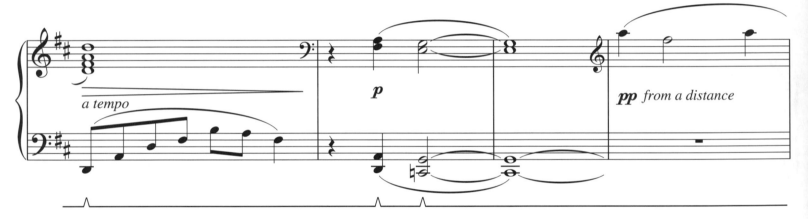

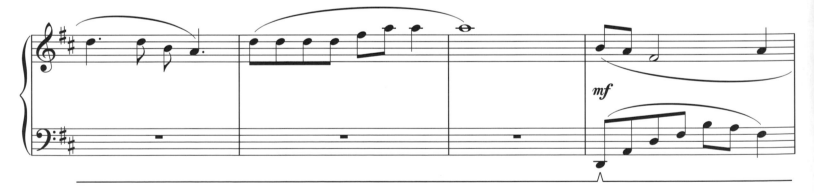

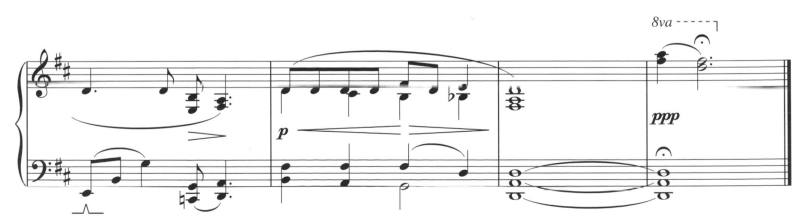